I0190897

Mary Shelley

Leslie Buffam

Explore other books at:
WWW.ENGAGEBOOKS.COM

VANCOUVER, B.C.

ℰ⟶ WWW.ENGAGEBOOKS.COM

Mary Shelley: Level 2
Remarkable People
Leslie Buffam 1949 –
Text © 2023 Engage Books
Design © 2023 Engage Books

Edited by: A.R. Roumanis, Melody Sun,
Ashley Lee & Sarah Harvey
Design by: Mandy Christiansen

Text set in Arial Regular.
Chapter headings set in Fibra One Alt.

FIRST EDITION / FIRST PRINTING

LIBRARY AND ARCHIVES CANADA CATALOGUING IN PUBLICATION

Title: Mary Shelley / Leslie Buffam.
Names: Buffam, Leslie, author.
Description: Series statement: Remarkable People

Identifiers: Canadiana (print) 20230459986 | Canadiana (ebook) 20230459994
ISBN 978-1-77878-321-0 (hardcover)
ISBN 978-1-77878-322-7 (softcover)
ISBN 978-1-77878-323-4 (epub)
ISBN 978-1-77878-324-1 (pdf)
ISBN 978-1-77878-345-6 (audio)

Subjects:
LCSH: Shelley, Mary Wollstonecraft, 1797-1851—Juvenile literature.
LCSH: Women novelists, English—19th century—Biography—Juvenile literature.
LCSH: Novelists, English—19th century—Biography—Juvenile literature.
LCSH: Shelley, Mary Wollstonecraft, 1797-1851. Frankenstein—Juvenile literature.
LCGFT: Biographies.

Classification: LCC PR5398 .B84 2023 | DDC J823/.7—DC23

This project has been made possible in part
by the Government of Canada.

Canada ◆

Contents

Who Was Mary Shelley?

Mary Wollstonecraft Shelley was a **romantic** writer. She lived from 1797 to 1851.

KEY WORD

Romantic: a style of art that is about feelings and nature.

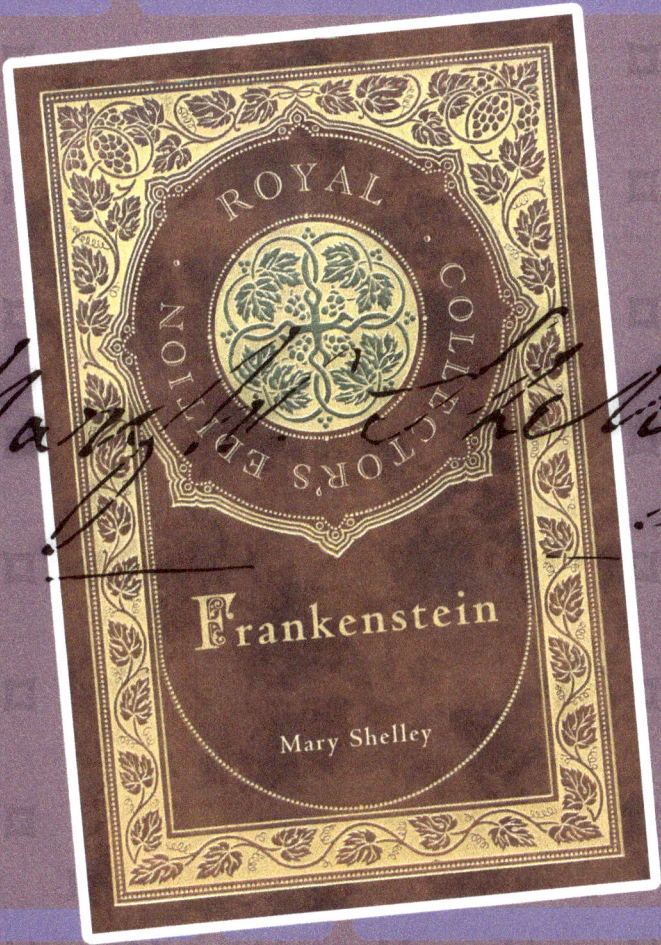

Mary started writing when she was just a child. She wrote her most famous work when she was only 18. It is called *Frankenstein*.

Early Life

Mary was born in England on August 30, 1797. Her parents were Mary Wollstonecraft and William Godwin. They were both writers.

Mary's mother died eleven days after Mary was born.

Mary's father married Mary Jane Clairmont in 1801. Mary did not get along with her stepmother.

Education

As a child, Mary went to a **dame-school**. She also spent seven months at a boarding school. This is a kind of school that students live in.

KEY WORD

Dame-school: a school that is run by a woman in her own home.

Mary was mostly taught at home by her father. She also learned a lot by listening and talking to her father's friends.

Many of William Godwin's friends were also writers.

England During Mary Shelley's Childhood

Mary grew up during a time when **factories** were starting to become popular. People stopped making products by hand.

KEY WORD

Factories: places where machines are used to make things people can buy.

Factory owners made lots of money. But they did not pay their workers very much.

Mary's Work

Mary wrote books, poems, essays, and plays for the theater. Mary made up many of her stories. She also wrote a lot about her travels.

During Mary's time, many people thought women were not smart enough to write about **politics**. Mary wrote about them anyway.

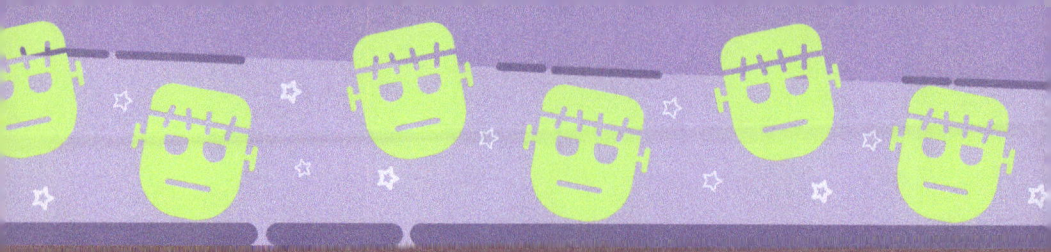

Frankenstein

Mary wrote *Frankenstein* in 1816. She and her friends were stuck inside because of cold weather. They decided to write ghost stories to tell each other.

Frankenstein is about a scientist who tries to make the perfect human but fails.

When Mary **published** *Frankenstein* in 1818, she did not put her name on the book. Many people thought it was written by a man.

KEY WORD

Published: made information available to people.

Mary's Travels

In 1814, Mary went on a six-week tour through France, Switzerland, Germany, and Holland. She wrote about this trip in her book called *History of a Six Weeks' Tour*.

Mary went on this trip with her future husband.

In 1818, Mary traveled to Italy. She returned to England in 1823. Mary wrote two books and two plays during this time.

Interests and Influences

Mary's father thought it was important for her to think for herself. He **encouraged** Mary to learn lots and use her imagination.

Women were not often encouraged to think for themselves in the 1800s.

Mary loved to read. She read most of what her parents had written. This helped shape her ideas about the world.

Personal Life

Mary married a poet named Percy Bysshe Shelley in 1816. They helped each other become better writers.

Mary and Percy had four children together. Only their oldest son lived to be an adult. Percy died in 1822.

MARCHMONT ASSOCIATION

Percy Bysshe Shelley
1792–1822
Poet & Radical Thinker
&
Mary Shelley
1797–1851
Author of Frankenstein
lived in a house
on this site
1815–16

After Percy died, Mary worked hard to make sure people knew about his work.

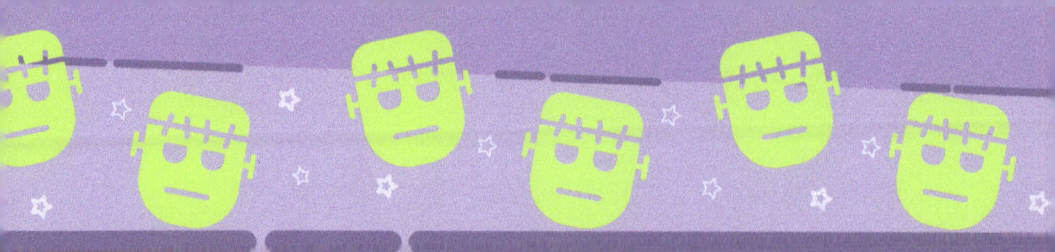

Legacy as a Writer

Frankenstein is thought to be the first **science fiction** book to be written in English. Science fiction is one of the most popular kinds of books.

KEY WORD

Science fiction: stories about the science and technology of the future that are made up.

Frankenstein is still read by many people today. It is often studied in schools.

When Mary was writing *Frankenstein*, the word "scientist" had not been invented yet.

IT'S TRUE!
Facts About Mary Shelley

The idea for *Frankenstein* came from a nightmare Mary had.

Mary published her first poem at the age of 14.

Mary's letters to Percy and her friends are available for people to read.

ESSAYS,
LETTERS FROM ABROAD,
TRANSLATIONS AND FRAGMENTS,
BY
PERCY BYSSHE SHELLEY.
EDITED
BY MRS. SHELLEY.

IN TWO VOLUMES.
VOL. II.

LONDON:
EDWARD MOXON, DOVER STREET.

Mary could read English, French, Latin, Greek, Italian, and some Spanish.

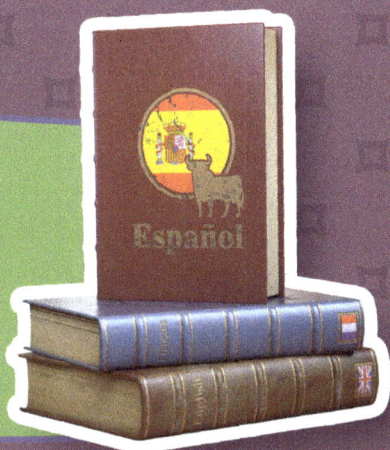

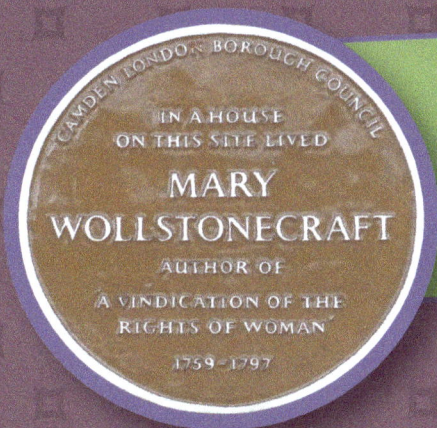

IN A HOUSE
ON THIS SITE LIVED

MARY
WOLLSTONECRAFT

AUTHOR OF

'A VINDICATION OF THE
RIGHTS OF WOMAN'

1759 - 1797

CAMDEN LONDON BOROUGH COUNCIL

Mary would often read at her mother's grave as a child.

Young Mary was once caught hiding behind a couch at night, listening to her father's friend read a poem he wrote.

TIMELINE

August 30, 1797
Mary Wollstonecraft Shelley is born

September 10, 1797
her mother dies

November 11, 1812
meets Percy Bysshe Shelley for the first time

February 22, 1815
her first daughter is born. She dies a few days later

December 30, 1816
marries Percy in London

1817
History of a Six Weeks' Tour is published

June 7, 1819
her son William dies in Rome

November 12, 1819
her fourth son, Percy Florence Shelley, is born

1801
her father marries Mary Jane Clairmont

1811
goes to Miss Petman's boarding school

January 1816
her second child, William, is born

June 1816
first writes *Frankenstein*

September 1817
her third child, Clara, is born. Clara dies a few weeks later

January 1, 1818
Frankenstein is published

July 8, 1822
Percy dies in Italy

February 1, 1851
dies at home in England at the age of 53

Be Like Mary Shelley

If you would like to be like Mary
- Use your imagination.
- Read lots of books.
- Learn other languages.

- Spend time with other artists and writers.
- Do what makes you happy.
- Believe in yourself.

Quiz

Test your knowledge of Mary Shelley by answering the following questions. The questions are based on what you have read in this book. The answers are listed on the bottom of the next page.

1 What kind of writer was Mary?

2 Did Mary write a lot about her travels?

3 What is *Frankenstein* about?

4 What did Mary's father encourage her to do?

MARCHMONT ASSOCIA
Percy Bysshe Shelley
1792–1822
Poet & Radical Thinker
&
Mary Shelley
1797–1851
Author of Frankenstein
lived in a house
on this site
1815–16

5 How many children did Mary and Percy have together?

6 At what age did Mary publish her first poem?

Explore other Readers.

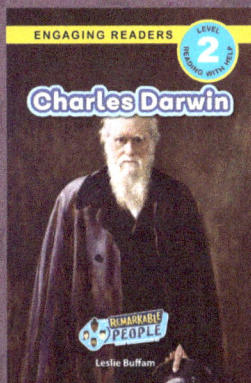

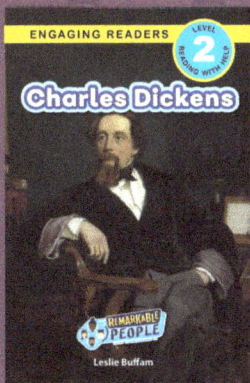

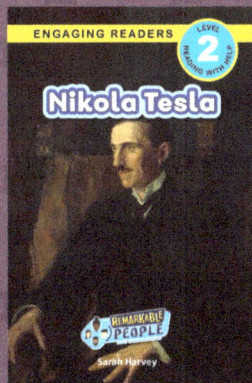

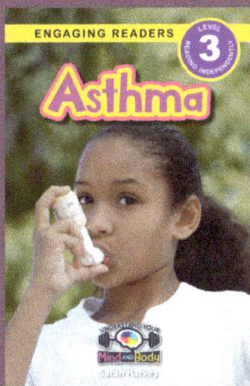

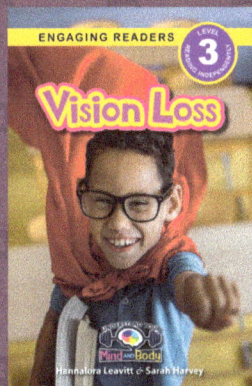

ENGAGING READERS — LEVEL 2 READING WITH HELP
Charles Darwin
REMARKABLE PEOPLE
Leslie Buffam

ENGAGING READERS — LEVEL 2 READING WITH HELP
Charles Dickens
REMARKABLE PEOPLE
Leslie Buffam

ENGAGING READERS — LEVEL 2 READING WITH HELP
Nikola Tesla
REMARKABLE PEOPLE
Sarah Harvey

ENGAGING READERS — LEVEL 3 READING INDEPENDENTLY
ADHD
Mind and Body
AJ Knight

ENGAGING READERS — LEVEL 3 READING INDEPENDENTLY
Asthma
Mind and Body
Sarah Harvey

ENGAGING READERS — LEVEL 3 READING INDEPENDENTLY
Diabetes
Mind and Body
Kit Caudron-Robinson

ENGAGING READERS — LEVEL 3 READING INDEPENDENTLY
Obesity
Mind and Body
Kit Caudron-Robinson

ENGAGING READERS — LEVEL 3 READING INDEPENDENTLY
Speech Disorders
Mind and Body
AJ Knight

ENGAGING READERS — LEVEL 3 READING INDEPENDENTLY
Vision Loss
Mind and Body
Hannalora Leavitt & Sarah Harvey

Visit www.engagebooks.com/readers

Answers: 1. A romantic writer 2. Yes 3. A scientist who tries to make the perfect human but fails 4. Learn lots and use her imagination 5. Four 6. Fourteen

www.ingramcontent.com/pod-product-compliance
Lightning Source LLC
Chambersburg PA
CBHW051238020426
42331CB00016B/3432